Sebastian's Super Special Secret

A book for kids with one agnostic parent and one of faith

Published by

Nightingale Rose Publications

16960 E. Bastanchury Rd. suite J

Yorba Linda, Ca. 92886

Acknowledgements

I want to extend my appreciation to Pareesa, Michael, Mason and Arman (at least his profile) for the generous gift of their time and enthusiasm in modeling for this book, and to Barbara and Tom for the lovely setting of their beautiful home. I also want to thank Baz for his expertise and patience in doing the creative design for this book and its cover and for helping me with the artwork. And big loving thank-yous to my sweetheart, Mike, for all his support and unending encouragement, setting up my workspace and for all the creative meals while I wrote, drew and edited this book. And appreciation to my children, Harry and Teddi, for modeling how acceptance is put into action in a world in need of tolerance.

Library of Congress Catalog Card Number:

1-6265365031

ISBN-13: 978-1-889755-09-0

ISBN-10: 1-889755-09-5

Disclaimer

This book is intended to provide information regarding the subject matter covered. It is not designed to take the place of professional counseling. If a child or an adult is experiencing signs of depression, severe anxiety reactions, or other psychological disturbances, it is important that they receive professional help. Licensed therapist in your area can be found online under "psychologists," "Counseling," or "Therapy."

My name is Sebastian. I have a super special family because we have a super special secret.

I bet you can't guess what our super special secret is.

I'll give you a hint.

Mom makes breakfast before Dad and I go to church. I learn stories about how people lived in the olden days.

When we come home, she asks about my Sunday School friends and snack time.

Want another hint?

On New Year's Eve we make popcorn and read our gratitude notes.

POP, POP, POP! I get extra butter on my popcorn!

YUM. YUMMY! YUM!

Sometimes I accidently get butter on my notes.

Last year we filled up the whole jar!

My last one said, "I'm grateful I'm getting a new baby brother…..or sister.

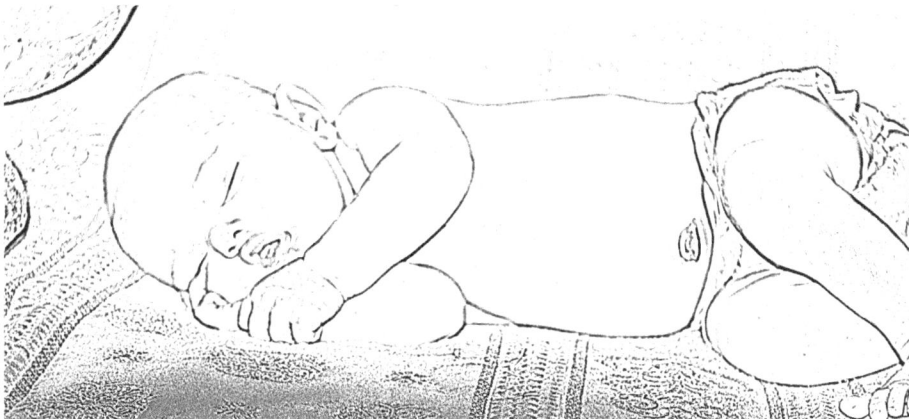

How about another hint?

My friend David plays video games in his room while he eats.
BING! ZING! TA DA!!

I asked if I could do that at my house. But Mom and Dad both said,
"Nope. No way, thanks for giving it a spin!"

We eat together at the table.

Mom says, "No screens, just beans."

Ruffy hopes I'll drop something. SNIF, SNIF, SNIF

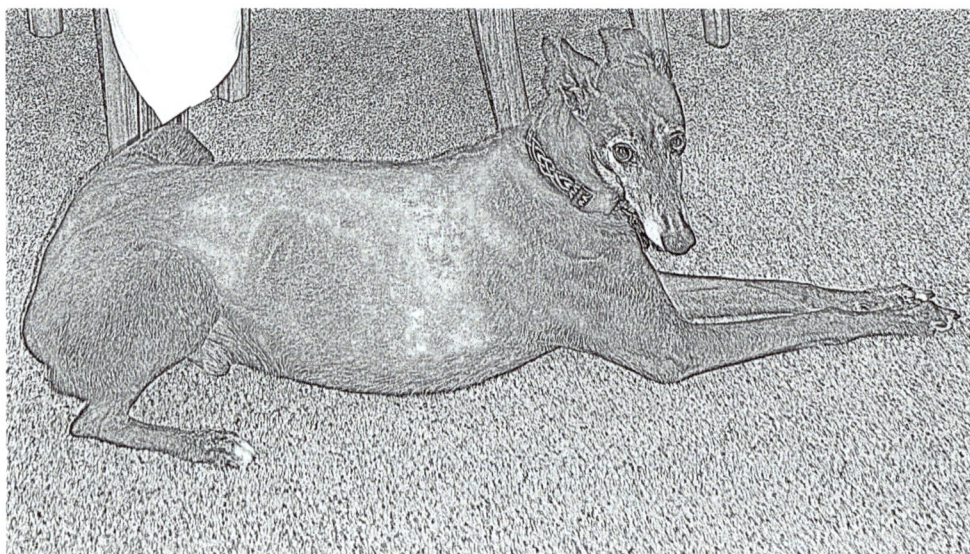

Before we eat Mom and Dad take turns talking.

Dad folds his hands and says grace. He asks God to bless our food and make our bodies strong.

When he says, "Amen," I make a big muscle and everyone smiles.

When Mom starts our meal, she talks about all the people who help bring us our food.

CLAP! CLAP! CLAP!

Farmers, HOE! HOE! HOE!

Ranchers, HE HAW! GIDDY UP!

Pickers, PLUCK! PLUCK! PLUCK!

Trucker drivers.

VROOM! VROOM! VROOM!

Grocery store cashiers.

CA-CHING! CA-CHING! CA-CHING!

Cooks.

CHOP! CHOP! CHOP!

And bakers.

ROLL-EM! ROLL-EM! ROLL-EM!

We all take turns thinking of helpers. Dad always says, "Train engineers."

TOOT! TOOT! TOOT!

I make jokes, so I say, "Polar bears that give us ice cream!"

We all pretend to shiver and laugh.

BRRRRRRRR! BRRRRRR! BRRRRRR!

I'll give you another hint about our super special secret.

We all like music. Mom likes Zydeco.

Dad like classic rock.

Mom sings me silly songs
while I brush my teeth.

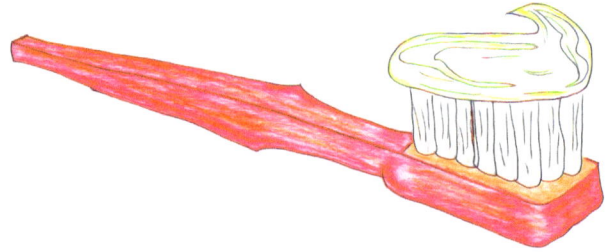

Dad sings holiday songs when we decorate.

I like it when they sing different. They call it, "harmony."

I play the drum and mom waves a flag.

BUH-DUM! BUH-DUM! BUH-DUM!

"Keep it down," Dad says. "You're making the windows rattle!"

Saturday nights we sing karaoke. They mix up the words, but I sing them right!

When they sing mushy songs I say, "OH, YUCK!"

But mom just smiles big when Dad sings her lovey-dovey songs.

I bet you're getting closer. How about one more hint?

Mom thinks religion has old-fashioned rules. Dad says when you love someone you want to follow their wishes.

We have five important rules in our home.

1. BE COURTEOUS.

That means when I ask for something I have to wait and listen, and not argue. Mom says it also means holding the door for her and saying, "Please" and "Thank you."

Dad says it means not taking other people's stuff and only wishing good things for them.

2. BE AUTHENTIC

This means "be real" and don't say things that aren't true. Don't try to show off or act like I'm better than someone else.

Dad says I'm still authentic when I wear costumes and make up plays.

Mom says people are brave when they're true to themselves.

Dad agrees.

NO POSERS, BE THE REAL DEAL.

3. BE KIND

This means be nice to everyone, even myself.

Dad says all religions teach we should treat other people the way we want them to treat us.

Mom agrees that everyone needs to be nice to each other.

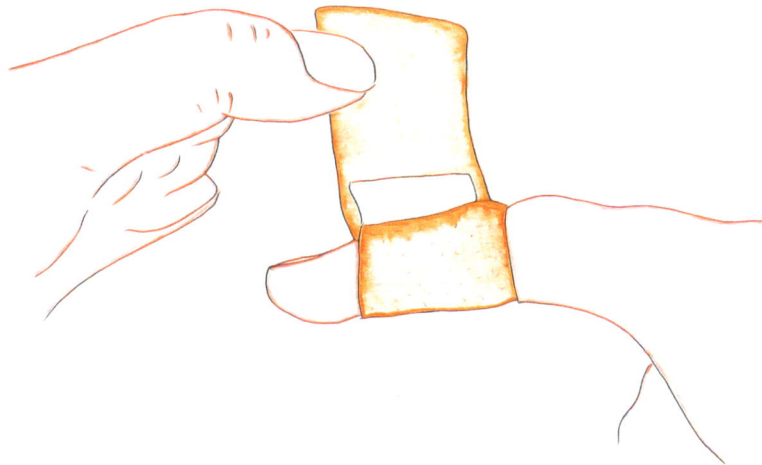

BE TWICE AS NICE, OR NO DICE, ICE!

4. SHOW RESPECT

This means I do things to help myself feel better when I'm angry. It means that I don't blame someone else when I feel bad or try to hurt them back.

It's really hard when I'm angry or scared!

DON'T GET EVEN, OWN YOUR FEELIN'

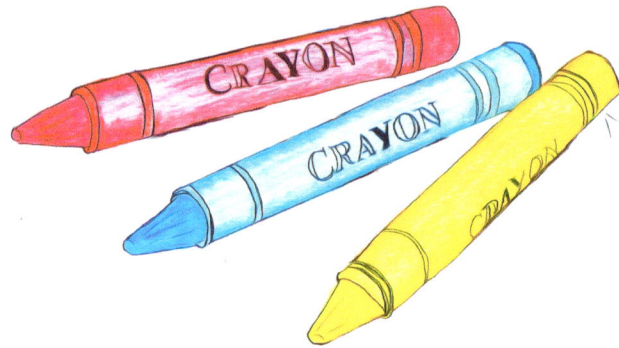

5. HELP OTHERS

I like this rule. I like helping set the table. We also collect bottles and cans.

We recycle and give the money to the homeless shelter.

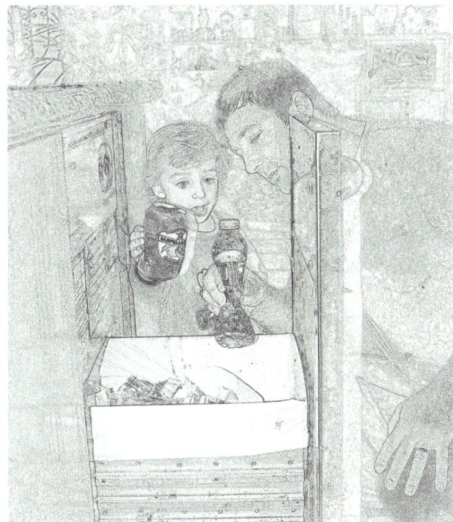

Sometimes we walk with lots of other people for things we care about.

At school I stick up for kids who get picked on. I never laugh if someone makes fun of other people or groups of people.

COME ON TAKE A STAND, LEND A HELPING HAND.

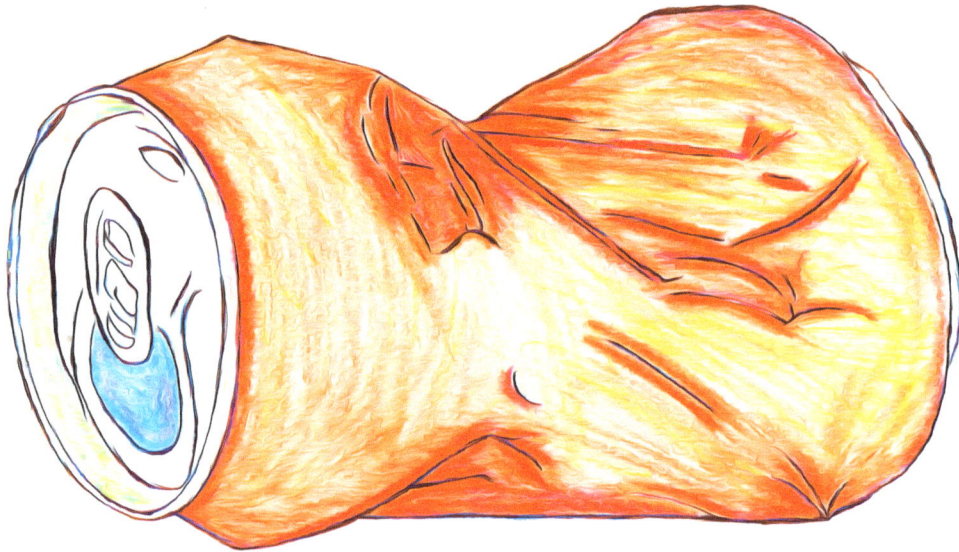

Those are our rules.

Want one more hint?

Mom and Dad both cried when Uncle Bobby died.

Dad says he's up in heaven now.

Mom says we'll carry him in our hearts forever, especially when we watch his favorite baseball team.

Uncle Bobby's picture is on a table. When we miss him we tell stories about him.

Dad lights a candle on Uncle Bobby's birthday and on holidays.

Mom writes down the score of every Cub's game and puts it on Uncle Bobby's table.

I cut out pictures that remind me of things I did with Uncle Bobby.

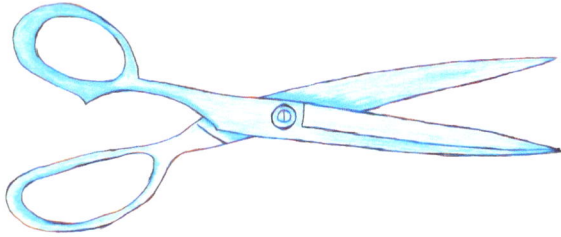

Dad says my collage is perfect for our memory table.

Mom and Dad both tell me to fill each day up with my best memories.

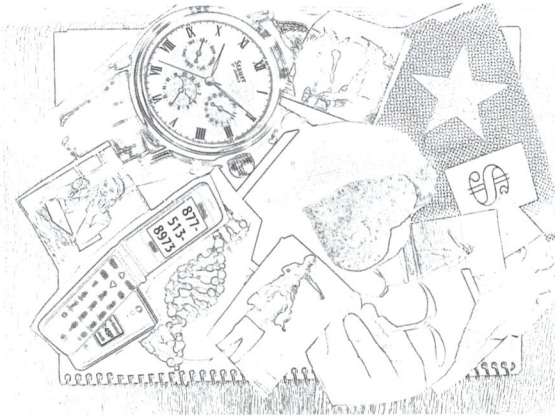

Dad believes in heaven. It's a happy place where people go after they die. He says we'll see them again someday.

Mom says no one can know for sure if that's true. She says, "There's no proof that heaven is real." She only believes what science can research.

I like that they don't talk to me like a little kid.

I bet you're getting really close to guessing our super special secret! I'll give you another hint.

We're going to have a new baby!

Mom says every time a baby is born life moves forward. She says it took millions of years for our special baby to be possible.

Dad says our baby is a gift from God.

I can't wait to see him…..or her.

I bet you'll guess our secret with this hint!

I don't ever want to go to bed. But I like it when Mom and Dad take turns tucking me in.

Dad reads me Bible stories. He sings me songs he learned as a kid. That was a LONG time ago!

I like hearing about miracles and how God protects kids.

Dad asks God to bless everyone we know, and then he kisses me good night.

When Mom puts me to bed she reads me fairytales from other countries. She uses funny voices. She growls at the bad guys. GRRRRRRRR!

She cheers for the heroes.

HOORAH! HOORAH!

Mom and I play a game. I point to a place on the globe, and she tells me how kids in that county go to sleep.

Most kids share a bed with other people in their family.

Then she sings me a lullaby and kisses me good night.

You know our super special secret now, huh?

Yep! We all love each other bigger than the whole universe!

My parents love each other so much, that they want us all to feel happy and safe. They don't try to change each other.

I want to have that kind of love when I grow up and get married.

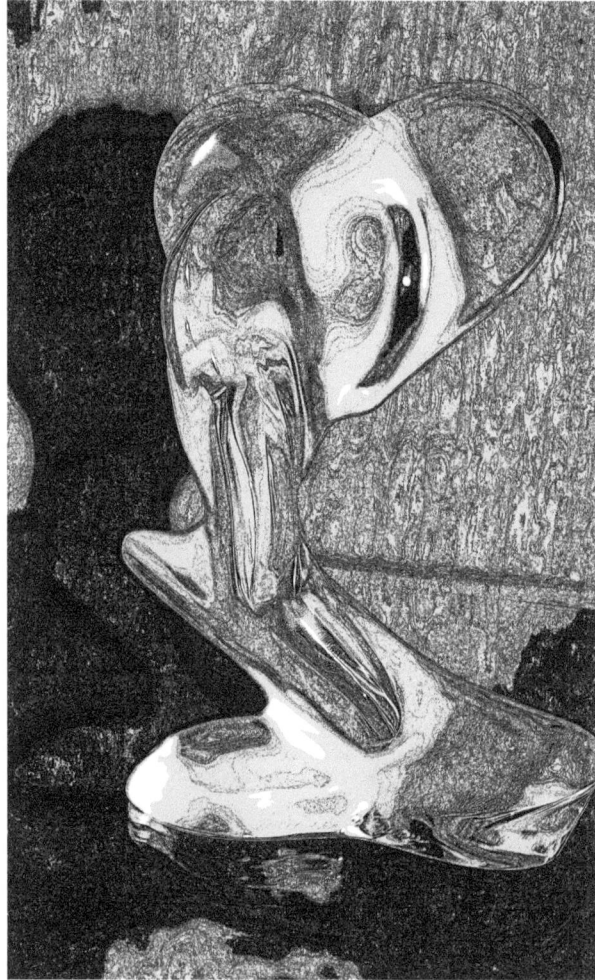

THE END.

www.ingramcontent.com/pod-product-compliance
Lightning Source LLC
LaVergne TN
LVHW072052070426
835508LV00002B/52